TO SAIL NO MORE

PART FOUR

IAN BUXTON

1

Breaking up the Royal Navy's warships

The 19th century saw the transition from wood to iron to steel in the construction of the Royal Navy's warships. At the end of their lives, wooden ships were of limited value. Somes fittings and upperworks might be removed, but much of the hull would be in poor condition. Any timber still in good condition could be salvaged, as could copper sheathing and metal fastenings. Such work was often done in the Royal Dockyards, sometimes in drydock, so a metal shipbreaking industry, as such, did not evolve in Britain until towards the end of the 19th century. However, the firm of Henry Castle had been established on the Thames in 1838, regularly purchasing 'wooden walls' for demolition at Millbank, later at Charlton and Woolwich. Sound teak and oak could be sold as such, or fashioned into furniture, particularly for outdoor use, although the rest was usually only firewood.

A handful of other dismantlers operated around the dockyard ports, but it was only when iron-built vessels began to be disposed of in any number that shipbreaking could become a significant commercial enterprise. Warship hulls now had an appreciable scrap value, since the material could be remelted. In particular the production of mild steel from the 1880s boosted demand, since the open hearth steel furnace required a proportion of scrap in its charge. From around 1890, a number of companies expanded into the shipbreaking business, including George Cohen and the well known Sheffield company Thomas W Ward, established in 1878, who opened their first yard at Preston in 1894. There were still not many iron warships being sold for scrap, since early vessels now of little military value were often converted into training vessels or accommodation hulks, their hulls still sound owing to the modest rate of corrosion of wrought iron. Thus breaking up warships was a somewhat fragmented business until into the 20th century, with only a handful of ships being sold for scrap each year.

The situation changed dramatically following Fisher's first appointment as First Sea Lord in October 1904. The Navy List had become inflated with obsolete vessels of little fighting value, yet the ships absorbed men and materials needed elsewhere. One hundred and fifty four vessels were removed from the effective list in 1905. Some were sold for use in non-military roles, but many were sold for scrap. The first auction of discarded vessels was held at Chatham Dockyard on 4 April 1905, the London "Times" reporting the following day that 29 ships had been sold for a total of £138,000.

These and subsequent sales prompted not only new companies to enter the shipbreaking business (such as Forth Shipbreaking at Boness, financed by P & W MacLellan of Glasgow in 1905) but also existing companies to expand. Ward's opened new yards at Morecambe in 1905 and at Briton Ferry in 1906, the latter close to the South Wales steel industry, which lacked the iron ore supplies of the more northerly works. These yards were laid out with substantial jetties, sheerlegs and steam cranes (later electric), good rail access and a beaching ground to finish off hulks at low tide. The oxy-acetylene cutter began to appear, but used initially only for thick or awkward sections of the hull, hand 'unbuttoning' of riveted structure with hammer and chisel still being the norm, given the then relative costs of labour and gas. Markets were developed in second-hand machinery, equipment and furniture. A steady stream of warships proceeded to be broken up in British yards. Hughes Bolckow and John Cashmore, both already in the steel business, entered shipbreaking around 1909, respectively on the Tyne (Blyth from 1912) and at Newport. Shipbreaking effectively ceased during World War 1 other than for the recovery of scrap from damaged vessels or a few wooden craft.

Following the Armistice in November 1918, it was clear that there would be a huge surplus of naval vessels. With the heavy WW1 building programme, almost every vessel built before about 1910 was redundant. The Admiralty began to sell off vessels from the spring of 1919. Shipbreaking companies mushroomed, with ships being sold at giveaway prices to clear the dockyards. This encouraged organizations who had little idea about the techniques of ship demolition or how to get the best price for recovered material. The established companies also expanded rapidly, surveying sites for new yards. Ward's, for example, opened ten new yards between 1919 and 1922 including Barrow, Grays and Inverkeithing.

By the mid-1920s, the surge of surplus naval vessels had dropped off, and most of the amateur breakers had retired from the scene. The remaining breakers survived to the early 1930s when the shipping slump encouraged more newcomers, including shipbuilding companies, to enter shipbreaking to handle surplus merchant vessels. After three British battleships including MARLBOROUGH had gone for scrap in the early 1930s, there were relatively few warships scrapped, the RN having already been run down to a low level. Metal Industries broke up at Rosyth all the German capital ships salvaged from Scapa Flow, like BAYERN in 1935. The only other significant group of warships sold was the 34, mainly destroyers, which the Admiralty handed over to Ward's in 1936 in part exchange for the liner MAJESTIC, which they wished to convert into the training ship CALEDONIA.

Until the end of WW2, virtually no more British warships were scrapped. Then, as explained in Part 1 of this book, from 1940 to 1962, ships were scrapped under the BISCO system, not sold to shipbreakers, but 'handed over' for demolition. The net proceeds from sale of scrap materials, less breaking and other costs, was later returned to the appropriate government Ministry, in effect a deferred sale price.

The figures for three typical BISCO vessels are shown below.

NEWCASTLE Town class cruiser. 9100 tons standard displacement. Completed 1937. Arrived Shipbreaking Industries' yard at Faslane 19 August 1959. Demolition completed June 1961.

	Tons	Av £/ton	£
Steel scrap	5782	11.2	64,758
Armour scrap	1067	19.57	20,885
Non-ferrous	707	160.2	113,260
Re-usables, sundries and oil	350	32.46	11,362
Total sales	**7906**	**26.66**	**210,265**
Demolition costs		6.70	52,986
Towage, carriage etc			15,155
Total costs		8.62	68,141
Net proceeds		**17.98**	**142,124**

NEWCASTLE's sale value if auctioned would thus have been about £140,000, depending on the anticipated scrap material prices and expected profit margin, or £15.38 per ton of standard displacement.

OXFORD CASTLE Castle class frigate. 1060 tons standard displacement. Completed 1944. Arrived T W Ward's yard at Briton Ferry 6 September 1960. Demolition completed June 1962.

	Tons	Av £/ton	£
Steel scrap	765	11.23	8,593
Non-ferrous	53	150.9	7,997
Re-usables, sundries and oil	20	42.1	842
Total sales	**838**	**20.80**	**17,432**
Demolition costs		6.48	5,428
Towage, carriage etc			1,575
Total costs		8.35	7,003
Net proceeds		**12.45**	**10,429**

OXFORD CASTLE's sale value if auctioned would have been about £10,000 or £9.43 per ton of standard displacement.

TELEMACHUS T class submarine. 1090 tons standard displacement. Completed 1943. Arrived Shipbreaking Industries' yard at Charlestown 25 August 1961. Demolition completed December 1962.

	Tons	Av £/ton	£
Steel scrap	636	11.7	7,107
Non-ferrous	105	165.8	17,414
Re-usables, sundries and oil	2	27.5	55
Total sales	**743**	**33.08**	**24,576**
Demolition costs		7.25	5,390
Towage, carriage etc			797
Total costs		8.32	6,187
Net proceeds		**24.74**	**18,389**

TELEMACHUS' sale value if auctioned would have been about £18,000 or £9.43 per ton of standard displacement. Her battery had already been removed.

The pocket in 3 Basin at Portsmouth dockyard has long been used for discarded ships. In this photograph taken on 3 August 1959 can be seen the incomplete carrier LEVIATHAN (towed from the Tyne in July 1946) and LST 3522 TRACKER (in use as a harbour accommodation vessel for VICTORIOUS during her modernisation). Beyond lies TRIUMPH, whose conversion to a repair ship had been suspended. The two cruisers outboard are MAURITIUS in Operational Reserve and NEWFOUNDLAND, shortly before her sale to Peru.

A unique sight in the Gareloch on 15 November 1946, with the scuttled German battlecruiser DERFFLINGER upside down in the former Admiralty Floating Dock No. 4. Metal Industries (MI) had raised her at Scapa Flow in July 1939, but the outbreak of WW2 prevented them from breaking her up in drydock at Rosyth Dockyard, as they had with the other salvaged German capital ships. She lay throughout the war at Lyness, floating upside down on a cushion of compressed air. MI were not able to use the Rosyth drydocks after WW2, but were permitted to lease No. 1 Military Port at Faslane in the Gareloch and purchase AFD.4. The hulk was towed from Lyness to the Clyde, arriving on 12 September 1946. She was then manoeuvred into AFD.4, which would form her cradle for demolition.
In the background are eight LST 3s, (including 3044, 3520 and 3523) and two LCT 8s.

6 VANGUARD on 3 August 1956 on the River Tamar - not long out of a £220,000 refit at Devonport and shortly before she became flagship of the Reserve Fleet at Portsmouth. HOWE behind her had been laid up since 1952.

The northern part of the Gareloch provided moorings for several of the RN's largest laid up vessels. Three KING GEORGE V class battleships are visible in this view of 14 April 1956, ANSON nearest, KGV behind her stern and DUKE OF YORK far right. The incomplete carrier HERCULES lies between, awaiting her move to Belfast to be fitted out as the Indian VIKRANT.

Left to right in the Gareloch on 9 June 1956 are KING GEORGE V, the cruiser SWIFTSURE awaiting her abortive modernisation at Chatham and HERCULES. Just visible, alongside at Faslane, lies the depot ship WOOLWICH acting as HQ ship of the Clyde Reserve Fleet, HMS JUPITER.

At the south end of the Gareloch above Rhu Narrows lies the ex training carrier INDEFATIGABLE on 14 April 1956. Her low 14 ft hangars precluded economical conversion to a more modern carrier, so she was towed away on 4 November 1956 to be broken up at Dalmuir. L.3031 lies beyond her bows.

9

Fountain Lake between Portsmouth Dockyard and Whale Island has long been used for laid up warships. Here on 3 August 1957, sixteen inshore minesweepers are berthed on the cruiser GLASGOW, with LIVERPOOL beyond. The nearest uncanopied IMS is M2777 WINTRINGHAM.

In Fareham Creek on 3 August 1957 lie the cruisers DIDO (nearest) and CLEOPATRA, flagship of the Reserve Fleet until replaced by VANGUARD in November 1956. Both were towed to the breakers the following year, where they realised net sums of £72,380 and £82,851 respectively, after deducting all breaking costs - about 7% of their construction cost new, excluding armament.

A wide variety of vessels is shown here (on 3 August 1956) at the Reserve Fleet trots in the Hamoaze between Devonport Dockyard and Saltash Bridge. Nearest is the Algerine class minesweeper ROMOLA, berthed on the cruiser BELLONA, then EURYALUS, forming the Plymouth Reserve Fleet base HMS ORION.

Further south along the trot on 3 August 1956 is the maintenance carrier UNICORN, which was placed in reserve in 1953 after service in the Korean War. She was eventually towed away to the Clyde for scrapping in June 1959 (see page 54). The cruisers are BELLONA and EURYALUS.

UNICORN reveals her unusual open stern on 3 August 1956, designed to allow overhauled aircraft engines to be tested in the open. The repair ship ALAUNIA lies in the next trot, operating as a training vessel for stoker mechanics.

At the head of the Hamoaze trots also on 3 August 1956 lies the ALAUNIA, a former Cunarder. Alongside her is the former WW1 monitor MARSHAL NEY as the tender ALAUNIA II, stripped of her armament and barely recognisable under the hutments on deck. The Battle class destroyer SLUYS provided practical experience of modern steam turbine machinery for the trainees. UNICORN lies astern.

The cruiser GAMBIA in Fareham Creek on 12 March 1967. She had an extensive refit at Rosyth 1956-57, but was laid up at Portsmouth in reserve from the end of 1960. Page 28 in Part 2 of this book shows her leaving for Inverkeithing on 2 December 1968; see also page 62.

Left: Barry was one of several South Wales ports used to disperse Reserve Fleet ships in the 1950s. Here on 12 August 1956 are two Battle class destroyers, GRAVELINES (inboard) and ST JAMES, both in Operational Reserve

Right: An unusual collection of vessels at Portsmouth Dockyard on 3 August 1959. The navigational training vessel REDPOLE (outboard) is the only one in commission. D129 TARIQ was the name adopted by Pakistan when the destroyer OFFA was transferred in 1949; she was shortly to be towed to Sunderland for scrapping. D27 SAVAGE is in Extended Reserve (ER), while beyond her lies the Hunt class BRECON, also in ER.

Two Type 2 Hunts lie outboard of two Type 3s at Hartlepool on 8 April 1956. Furthest outboard is AVON VALE (at Hartlepool mid 1953 to May 1958), BLANKNEY (mid 1953 to March 1959), TALYBONT (January 1953 to end 1956) and HAYDON (November 1955 to May 1958).

Three different lengths of escort at Hartlepool on 16 August 1959: the destroyer OBEDIENT (345 ft, Operational Reserve), Hunt class FARNDALE (282 ft, Supplementary Reserve) and minesweeper MUTINE (225 ft, OR). The white mark at the waterline at each bow is a "telltale" to show if a laid-up ship is taking on water.

Three Algerine class minesweepers at Hartlepool 18 August 1957. Left is PROVIDENCE (at Hartlepool mid 1953 to May 1958), then ALBACORE (October 1956 to September 1963) and MARMION (1952 to March 1959). Alongside berthing was more economical than being moored in the stream; access was easier for maintenance and shore power was available. Ships would be occasionally drydocked, e.g. MARMION at Hull in 1956.

Reserve Fleet ships had been laid up at Hartlepool since 1952. Ten years later in June 1962, the small naval party looking after them is seen here on board their HQ ship LOCH TRALAIG, about to leave with the closure of the base. The cap tallies read HMS DUNCANSBY HEAD, the accommodation ship at Rosyth - and accounting base for the Hartlepool ships.

Reserve ships at Barrow came under HMS ORION, the Plymouth Command Reserve Fleet, but the local HQ ship was the frigate BALLINDERRY. Photographed on 3 October 1957 she shows off the pleasing lines of the River class. She was handed over to Ward's yard at the north end of Devonshire Dock on 7 July 1961, the site now covered by BAE SYSTEMS (ex Vickers) construction hall.

After WW2, surplus ships were laid up wherever berths could be found, in estuaries such as the Stour at Harwich. Little effort was made to protect the ships, a token funnel cover sufficing. Still bearing their wartime pendant numbers in October 1948 are the destroyers NOBLE (nearest), PENN and ESKIMO. The latter was scrapped at Troon the following year, one of the last British Tribal class to arrive at the breakers yard on 2 June. PENN also went to Troon in 1950. NOBLE, ordered as NERISSA (but named PIORUN when Polish manned 1940-46), moved to the Medway before being scrapped at Dunston in 1955. (M Crowdy, World Ship Society)

Throughout most of the 1950s, surplus warships were laid up in the River Medway, both in creeks above Sheerness and off St Mary's Island, north of the Chatham Dockyard basins. Off the latter, two Hunts are seen on 6 August 1956, MELBREAK nearest and BICESTER. Both were soon to be towed to Ward's scrapyard at Grays, Essex, the former arriving on 22 November and the latter on 23 August.

The Hamoaze (Devonport) trots on 3 August 1956 show some of the smaller vessels laid up. Nearest is the River class HELMSDALE, having been used for propeller trials, and beyond her, funnels of ever decreasing size can be made out, reflecting the less powerful engines of: minesweeper PYRRHUS, trawler SHEPPEY and controlled minelayer REDWING.

A pair of Bangor minesweepers at Harwich in October 1948. Nearest is POLRUAN, her condition such that she went to Sunderland for scrap in June 1950. Canadian built FORT YORK is in better condition and was sold to become the Portuguese COMMANDANTE ALMEIDA CARVALHO - perhaps there was a problem finding space on such a small ship to display a name of that length! (M Crowdy, World Ship Society)

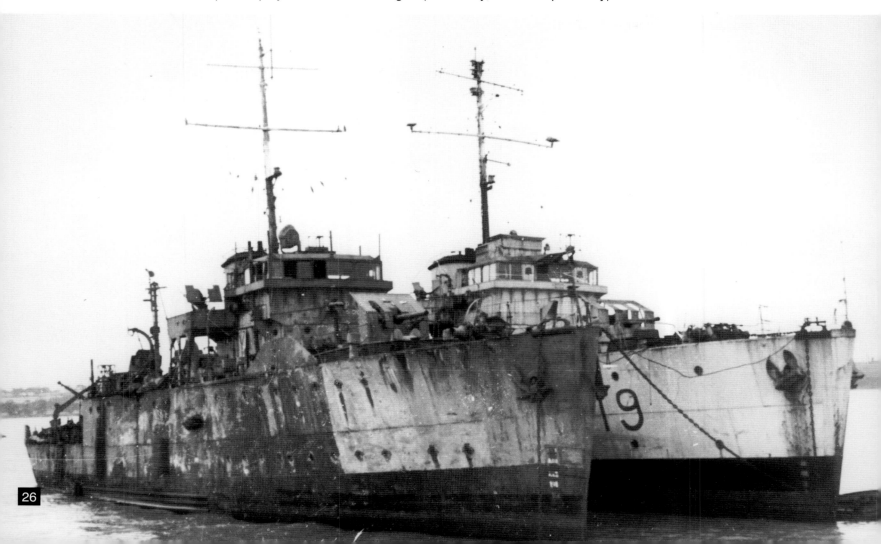

Fareham Creek in Portsmouth Harbour on 20 March 1966, with TALLY-HO nearest, still with her gun and external torpedo tubes, as one of the partly welded but unmodernised T class. She was scrapped at Briton Ferry the following year, being sold for £23,300. Astern are MEON, LOCH KILLISPORT and LOCH LOMOND.

More of the Fareham Creek mothball fleet on 20 March 1966, with the Type 15 frigate ROCKET, nearest, sold to Arnott Young twelve months later for £48,000, LOCH RUTHVEN, left, who went to Davies & Cann at Plymouth and TRAFALGAR right, not scrapped until 1970 at Dalmuir.

The ex River class frigate MEON, latterly Amphibious Warfare Squadron HQ ship, in Fareham Creek 20 March 1966. She was in the process of being sold to Hughes Bolckow at Blyth for £40,000. She arrived on 14 May.

A year later on 12 March 1967, the line-up in Fareham Creek had changed. The ex radar picket destroyer CROSSBOW was being used by HMS SULTAN for harbour training. On the left can be seen the sterns of the destroyers LAGOS and CARRON, and to the right the LST MESSINA.

The Loch class frigate LOCH LOMOND in Fareham Creek on 12 March 1967. She had returned from the Far East in December 1964, going straight into reserve at Portsmouth. Curiously, she was towed to Chatham later in 1967, before being scrapped at Faslane in October 1968. Ahead of her is BROCKLESBY.

At the head of the trot on 12 March 1967 is the Hunt class BROCKLESBY, laid up after being sonar trials vessel until 1963. She was sold to Shipbreaking Industries at Faslane for £25,276 on 21 October 1968, where she yielded a profit of £1725 from 707 tons of scrap material. Astern lies LOCH LOMOND.

The south western wall of Rosyth Dockyard was host to all sorts of redundant ships. Here on 16 May 1959 is the repair ship ARTIFEX (ex Cunarder AURANIA), latterly artificer training ship, with the destroyer CONCORD alongside with the Hunt class TALYBONT, as part of HMS CALEDONIA.

The peacetime Royal Navy could not support in regular service the large minesweeper construction programme of the 1950s. HMS DILIGENCE at Hythe was the base at which many coastal minesweepers were laid up under their "Noah's Ark" canopies. United States Lines' AMERICA passes down Southampton Water on 23 September 1958, passing; left HUBBERSTON, centre CUXTON and right INVERMORISTON.

The 126-foot motor minesweepers proved useful as RNVR tenders in the 1950s, until replaced by the new Ton class coastal minesweepers. M.1038 was not so used, having been loaned to Denmark after WW2 until 1951. After service in the 51st Minesweeping Squadron, she went into reserve at Lowestoft, before moving to the Medway, where she is seen on 2 April 1956. Discarded in 1959, her hulk was slowly dismantled at Gillingham, surviving until at least 1965.

VANGUARD begins her 620 nautical mile voyage to the breaker's yard on 4 August 1960, headed towards Portsmouth Harbour entrance by ANTIC (left) and CAPABLE. The carrier THESEUS is at far left. Parts 1 and 2 of this book show views of her aground at the harbour entrance shortly after this photograph was taken.

Five days later on 9 August, VANGUARD is manoeuvred up the Gareloch by Steel & Bennie tugs, who took over from the deep sea tugs SAMSONIA and ADVICE at the Tail of the Bank in the Clyde approaches.

Two views from VANGUARD's fore masthead soon after she berthed at Shipbreaking Industries' Faslane yard on 9 August 1960. BISCO had paid £560,000 for her.

VANGUARD's 15-inch guns in the foreground were among the first pieces removed by the shipbreaker. She eventually yielded 38,800 tons of saleable material. (TW Ferrers-Walker)

The 6-inch roof plates from VANGUARD's 15-inch turrets had to be removed before the breech ends could be lifted out. Armour plates are numbered, so that they could be sold with a guaranteed chemical analysis, including the all-important nickel content. Y turret guns have already been removed on 4 September 1960, but X turret's have yet to be lifted out by the breakers floating crane.
(TW Ferrers-Walker)

The last of the Royal Navy's battleships VANGUARD makes her final voyage on 2 April 1962. Clyde Shipping's tug FLYING DUCK assists her hulk from the deepwater berth at Faslane to the beaching ground. Inset, the last section of engine room double bottom lies on a rail wagon in June 1962. (T W Ferrers-Walker)

KING GEORGE V made her last voyage of 12 nautical miles on 20 January 1958, from Tail of the Bank to Dalmuir. She had been moved from her Gareloch moorings on 8 January. Three Steel & Bennie tugs lead her past Dumbarton Castle.

Two views of KGV's superstructure as she is edged alongside at Dalmuir on 20 January 1958. All close range armament has already been removed, possibly at her last drydocking in Liverpool in 1955.

With decks covered in snow, KGV is eased into Arnott Young's basin at Dalmuir - built originally as the fitting out basin for Beardmore's new shipyard in 1905. The net proceeds of her demolition amounted to £467,065, i.e. the value of materials recovered minus the cost of demolition.

DUKE OF YORK's final voyage was only a couple of miles from her Gareloch mooring to Shipbreaking Industries' yard at Faslane on 18 February 1958. These two masthead views on 1 March show her as yet untouched. The liner hulk ahead is ASTURIAS. The net proceeds of her demolition amounted to £543,499, the highest of the four KGVs.

ANSON reveals her port side armour structure on 28 May 1958. The 6-inch deck armour at main deck level (one below the upper deck) is marked NC for non-cemented armour, the more ductile chromium-molybdenum alloy used on decks to deflect projectiles, compared with the hard faced cemented side armour. The hexagonal bolts secure the 15-inch side armour to the shell plating with teak backing between. An L shaped section is about to be lifted off by the 60-ton floating crane seen in the background. 11,939 tons of armour quality scrap was eventually recovered from ANSON. (TW Ferrers-Walker)

HOWE finally berths at Ward's Inverkeithing yard on 4 June 1958, after an ignominious three days spent aground and waiting for the fog to clear. United Towing's WELSHMAN (ex Admiralty GROWLER) helps manoeuvre her alongside the submarine depot ship MONTCLARE. United Towing had provided their tugs WELSHMAN and ENGLISHMAN (seen astern) to tow her from Devonport on 27 May for £10,000

This aerial view of Inverkeithing in July 1958 shows newly arrived frigate LARGO BAY alongside HOWE, with MONTCLARE inboard at the deep water berth. The tanker at No.1 berth ahead of HOWE is ANGLIAN CONFIDENCE.

RODNEY passes under the Forth railway bridge on 26 March 1948 on her final voyage from Rosyth to Inverkeithing. She had already been lightened by the removal of her six twin 6-inch turrets, and removal of all but one anchor and cable.

Ward's official photographer made several visits to Inverkeithing while the battleships were under demolition in the late 1940s. RODNEY can be seen at the deepwater berth in August 1948 with 16-inch turret demolition commenced but the bridge structure still largely intact five months after arrival.

The massive construction of RODNEY's triple 16-inch turrets becomes evident in this view of August 1948. The circular barbette armour is 15 inches thick, the turret faces 16 inches, the sides and rear 9 inches, the roof 7.25 inches and the floor 3 inches thick. The breech end is seen inside the gunhouse proper, although at full 40° elevation, it disappears beneath the turret floor. The revolving weight amounted to 1480 tons.

The older 15-inch turrets of REVENGE at Inverkeithing, outboard of NELSON in August 1949. The barrels are being cut into shorter lengths suitable for lifting off by cranes smaller than Ward's 50-ton crane seen in the background. The small gunhouse ports show that REVENGE's guns never had their elevation increased from 20 to 30 degrees, as in the QUEEN ELIZABETHs. She had been towed from Devonport on 28 August 1948 by ENGLISHMAN, SEAMAN and SUPERMAN for £5250, arriving at Inverkeithing on 4 September.

FORMIDABLE at Ward's deepwater berth at Inverkeithing in May 1953, with demolition not yet started. Although only 13 years old, she was not worth modernising to handle jet aircraft. She had left Portsmouth in tow of ENGLISHMAN, TRADESMAN and SEAMAN on 7 May, arriving on the 12th. The tow cost £6000. She yielded 19,756 tons of saleable material producing net proceeds of £141,727.

UNICORN at Arnott, Young's yard on 4 July 1959, shortly after the demolition of her island had commenced. She had been towed from Devonport on 11 June by WELSHMAN and TRADESMAN for £4,500, arriving at Dalmuir on the 15th. She yielded 13,536 tons of saleable material, with net proceeds of £180,730. Why has CITY OF GRIMSBY been painted mirrorwise below her compass platform?

The former training carrier OCEAN at Faslane in June 1962, with her flight deck cut away to open up the former hangar . She had been laid up at Devonport in Extended Reserve from the end of 1957. A plan to convert her to a depot ship for fishing vessels fell through, so she was allocated to Shipbreaking Industries for demolition. She arrived on 6 May 1962 in tow of ADVICE, one of the last large vessels to be broken up under the BISCO system. She yielded 10,347 tons of saleable scrap (plus 1223 tons of debris and rubbish) when demolition was completed in December 1963. (T W Ferrers-Walker)

VICTORIOUS at Faslane about September 1969. Her modernisation at Portsmouth involved a total rebuild from the hangar deck up, taking from 1950 to 1958 to complete. The bulges added for buoyancy and stability can just be made out at the waterline. (T W Ferrers-Walker)

The Town class cruiser BIRMINGHAM at Inverkeithing on 21 September 1960 newly arrived from Devonport. Although allocated under the BISCO system, a firm price had been paid to the Admiralty of £146,000, instead of the previous system of return of net proceeds after demolition. 7,721 tons of saleable material produced gross revenue of £208,128, but after deducting the purchase price and breaking costs, the profit was only £2,283. She lies alongside the tanker BARKENTINE.

Two cruisers at Cashmore's yard at Newport, South Wales in December 1949. Left is AJAX having arrived on 13 November after spending a few days aground at the mouth of the River Usk. The submarine inboard is probably U.3017, an ex-German Type XXI, designated N.41 by the RN when allocated for trials. Right is the trials cruiser CUMBERLAND photographed on 21 November 1959, whose 8269 tons of saleable material yielded net proceeds of £139,390. (T W Ferrers-Walker)

Boness on the south bank of the River Forth had been used for shipbreaking since the turn of the century, despite ships having to berth bows in to the shingly beach, as there was no proper jetty. The cruiser LIVERPOOL arrived at P & W MacLellan's Bridgeness yard on 2 July 1958, having been towed from Portsmouth on 27 June by WELSHMAN for £4000. The tug then returned to Portsmouth to tow LIVERPOOL's sister GLASGOW to Blyth. This photo taken on 13 September 1958 shows her well sunk into the mud. Demolition has commenced forward, with a steam scotch derrick erected on the main deck. She yielded 7,922 tons of saleable material, with net proceeds of £145,026.

SUPERB had been laid up in the Gareloch since 1957 so the voyage to Dalmuir took only a few hours on 8 August 1960. She is seen here five days later alongside HIGHLAND MONARCH. She yielded 7,691 tons of saleable material, giving net proceeds of £128,655. Over half the revenue came from 777 tons of non-ferrous material. Her hulk was towed to Troon on 16 May 1961 for final demolition.

These on-board views of SUPERB on 13 August 1960 show her to be virtually unchanged from her 1945 completion appearance.

Ward's had bought the cruiser GAMBIA in November 1968 for £257,600. She is seen here alongside the ferry ARNHEM at their Inverkeithing yard on 28 December 1968, having arrived from Portsmouth on the 6th. She yielded 7,467 tons of saleable material with a value of £463,725, producing over £100,000 profit after demolition costs.

The cruiser LION at Inverkeithing on 25 May 1975, alongside WAVE CHIEF. She had been moved to Rosyth in 1973, to provide spare parts for her sister ships TIGER and BLAKE. Her unlit hull was a deathtrap below decks, with holes cut in her decks for removal of equipment. One high pressure turbine and condenser was sold to a South American navy, probably Peru for ex CEYLON or ex NEWFOUNDLAND. She had been sold on 12 February 1975 for £262,500, making her final voyage on 24 April. Some of her 3.5 inch thick radiation-free nickel steel armour was sold to Nuclear Enterprises at £105 per ton.

The fast minelayer ARIADNE at Dalmuir on 19 February 1965, having arrived from Devonport on the 14th. She had been in reserve ever since 1946, although kept well maintained until going on the Disposal List. Her three twin 40mm were a US pattern mount, stemming from her days with the US Pacific Fleet in 1944.

These two deck views on 19 February give an idea of ARIADNE's condition. She had been purchased by Arnott Young for £69,000. Her hulk was towed to Troon on 4 June 1965 to complete demolition.

The Battle class destroyer LAGOS and Type 16 frigate PETARD lying at
Boness on the Forth on 13 June 1967. Although LAGOS had arrived
from Portsmouth only a few days earlier, her forward twin 4.5-inch
mounting has already been removed. PETARD (from Devonport)
remains untouched, out of reach of the cranes, having been purchased
by P & W MacLellan for £37,600, LAGOS for £43,700. (P Munro)

Two T class submarines at Faslane in September 1963, TRENCHANT (outboard) and TUDOR. They had arrived from Chatham on 23 July, having been purchased by Shipbreaking Industries for £18,400 each. All of TUDOR's main compartments have been opened up to provide direct lifts for the quayside cranes. The breakers had to return her Type 129AR sonar dome and both of TRENCHANT's Type 183 underwater telephones to the Admiralty, for further use. 875 tons of saleable material was obtained from each boat. The tanker ESSO MANCHESTER lies ahead of them.

Many V and W class destroyers were laid up in the Forth from 1944 onwards, most being scrapped locally. At Brechin's yard at Granton just west of Leith are (left to right) VERSATILE, VICEROY and WOLFHOUND photographed on 26 September 1948. (T W Ferrers-Walker)

Two frigates on the beaching ground at Faslane on 30 November 1957; left is HELMSDALE, right ENARD BAY. The former had arrived from Devonport on 4 November and beached on the 14th, while the latter had arrived on 15 November and beached on the 20th. The hulk of Shaw Savill's MATAROA lies ahead of them.

Shipbreaking Industries' Faslane yard continued to be busy even after the construction of the Polaris submarine base (HMS NEPTUNE) had started at the southern end of the port. The far left view on 2 August 1965 shows the Type 15 frigate VIGILANT and carrier MAGNIFICENT alongside the recently reconstructed quay. VIGILANT and her sister VIRAGO had been bought as a pair for £98,380. They had been offered for sale on 28 April with the submarine TEREDO, had been inspected at Devonport on 18 May, and SI's tender accepted on 1 June. The ships were delivered on 4 June. The Admiralty had requested the return of some of their sonar equipment, including Type 162 outfits, but they were found to be beyond economical repair. The pair yielded £175,395, giving a combined profit of £21,237. VIGILANT's demolition was completed on 12 February 1966 and VIRAGO's on 24 March. MAGNIFICENT had a relatively short operational life. Commissioned into the Royal Canadian Navy on 7 April 1948 to replace WARRIOR, she was returned to the RN on 14 June 1957 and replaced by BONAVENTURE. SI inspected her at Devonport on 19-20 May 1965, and had their tender of £185,700 accepted on 2 July. She arrived at Faslane on 12 July. Her 10,814 tons of scrap materials produced £374,395 of sales and a profit of £70,392.

The bows of RFA tanker ENNERDALE provide a good view of WIGTOWN BAY (left) and WHADDON at Faslane on 2 May 1959. An overhead view of the two is on Pages 62-63 of Part One of this book. Ahead lies the hulk of the battleship DUKE OF YORK.

P & W MacLellan had an overspill yard at Carriden a mile east of their main Boness yard. There the Black Swan frigate NEREIDE lies outboard of the hulk of Hunt class BELVOIR on 4 June 1958. The former had been towed from Portsmouth on 9 May by MERCHANTMAN for £1500, arriving on the 13th. The latter had also been towed by MERCHANTMAN from Portsmouth for £1600, departing 17 October 1957, arriving on the 21st. NEREIDE was to yield net proceeds of £14,327 from saleable material of 1,012 tons.

Another Black Swan/Hunt pair on that same day, 4 June 1958, but at Charlestown on the north shore of the Forth, nearly opposite Boness. LEDBURY is inboard of SPARROW to the right. SPARROW departed from Portsmouth on 22 May towed by MASTERMAN for £1250, arriving on the 26th. On the outer wall, the minesweeper COQUETTE also awaits her fate, she was also towed from Portsmouth on 22 May by TRADESMAN in a joint tow.

What a Hunt looks like after twelve years in reserve at Portsmouth. LEDBURY at Charlestown on 4 June 1958 shows the bridge layout clearly, as well as kooncoted single Oerlikon mounts. The twin 4-inch and director have been removed. She had been towed from Portsmouth on 7 May by SUPERMAN for £1250, arriving on the 12th, but was later transferred to Shipbreaking Industries' nearby Rosyth yard on 1 July for demolition.

One of the two Type 4 Hunts designed by Thornycroft, BRISSENDEN arriving from Lisahally near Londonderry on 2 March 1965 in tow of WRESTLER. She had been purchased by Arnott Young for £28,940. On 9 October her hulk was moved a mile downstream to their Old Kilpatrick yard for final demolition. This had been the site of Napier & Miller's shipyard, which closed in 1930. It was re-opened in 1941 for Findlay to erect prefabricated landing craft.

Dalmuir had a warship in hand almost all the time throughout the 1960s. Here on 26 September 1967 are seen from her masthead the Battle class destroyer FINISTERRE and (astern) the cut down hulk of Type 15 frigate ROCKET. The latter had arrived in March from Portsmouth, costing Arnott Young £48,000 to purchase, while the former cost £45,000.

FINISTERRE had left Devonport on 9 June for her three day voyage in tow of REWARD, who had just delivered LAGOS to Boness.

The guided missile destroyer HAMPSHIRE makes her last voyage up the River Neath to Ward's yard at Briton Ferry on 28 April 1979, having been towed by AGILE from Chatham. Tenders had been called for on 29 December 1978, with Ward's bid of £147,000 being accepted on 2 March.

The Whitby class frigate SCARBOROUGH completed her RN service in 1973 but a projected sale to Ecuador that year fell through. In 1975 she was sold to Pakistan, who were then unable to find the funds for a proposed refit at Swan Hunter's. After lying at buoys in the Tyne for two years, she was sold by the Ministry of Defence (acting as agents for the Pakistan Navy) to Blyth Shipbreakers and Shiprepairers. This company had leased Blyth Harbour Commission's drydocks for shipbreaking. She is seen here arriving at Blyth on 31 August 1977, assisted by the Blyth tug MAXIMUS.

The Type 15 frigate ULSTER at Ward's Inverkeithing yard on 23 February 1981, having arrived on 2 November 1980. She had been purchased for £78,169 after final service as a harbour training ship at HMS RALEIGH Plymouth. Her stern is actually that of URCHIN, which had been removed from the latter to repair ULSTER's collision damage in 1966.

No.3 drydock at Blyth was used by a number of Sheffield companies from 1975 to 1982. Here the frigate PUMA has her topmast removed on 3 January 1977, and dumped in the bottom of the dock. She had arrived from Chatham on 10 December 1976 in tow of ROLLICKER.

Unrecognisable as a Battle class destroyer, MATAPAN arrives at Blyth on 11 August 1979. She had remained in reserve, mostly at Devonport, until selected for conversion as a sonar trials vessel. Her extensive conversion was carried out at Portsmouth Dockyard from 1968 to 1972. Until her "second career" as a trials vessel she spent more time under tow than at sea under her own power. In 1947 she spent just 80 hours at sea under her own power for trials then was towed to Devonport (from Sheerness) in August 1948. To Rosyth in March 1960 ....Back to Devonport in April 1961 before her final tow to Portsmouth in September 1968 for refit.

Demolition in No. 3 drydock at Blyth at last revealed what had been done to MATAPAN in her major - highly classified - rebuild. The false keel constructed under the main hull is believed to replicate a submarine hull with passive sonar array transducers behind the glass reinforced plastic panels. Also visible in this view taken on 10 September 1979, are her bilge keel, fin stabilisers and acoustic tiles attached to the hull.

Left: At MATAPAN's fore end, a different sonar array was fitted, believed to be the prototype Type 2016 active/passive later fitted to the Type 22 Broadsword class frigates. The line of her original bow section is visible at the bulkhead on Frame 4 in this view of 13 November 1979.

Right: No.2 drydock at Blyth was also occasionally used by Kitson Vickers for demolition. Here the wooden hull of the coastal minesweeper ASHTON is well "sawn down" on 2 September 1977. The largest open compartment is the engine room, with the twin Deltic engines removed, with the generator compartment ahead. The aluminium frames and fittings had a reasonable scrap value, but the mahogany planking was not of much use, Hughes Bolckow's former garden furniture making division at Blyth having closed.

MATAPAN shared her dock with CACHALOT, which had arrived from Devonport on 14 February 1980. As shown on Page 17 of Part II of this book, her fin had been removed before sale. Right shows her on 23 February, virtually untouched.

Left The photograph shows her on 2 April 1980 with most of the casing removed, exposing the escape chamber and, behind it, the torpedo loading hatch. About half the starboard side ballast tanks have been removed, leaving the pressure hull still intact.

One of the last frigates to be broken up in the UK was AURORA by Duddon Valley Shipbreakers at Millom, near Barrow. She and her sister EURYALUS had been acquired by Devonport Management Ltd for spares and equipment to be used in the refitting of other Leanders, a venture that turned out to be loss-making for DML. AURORA had been towed from Devonport on 16 July 1990 by ROBUST to be lightened at Barrow. She was then moved to the shallow port of Millom where she finally berthed on 6 September. A better view of EURYALUS (behind AURORA) is shown on page 94 of the first part of this book, taken on the same day - 6 April 1991.

The Flower class corvette BURDOCK (nearest) and Bangor class minesweeper VEGREVILLE at Ward's Hayle yard in Cornwall in August 1947. (M Crowdy, World Ship Society)

The former salvage vessel KINLOSS on 11 July 1990 at R & M Supplies (Inverkeithing) Ltd's yard at Inverkeithing, owned by T W Ward until 1983 and then sold to James A White and then to R&M. Her sister UPLIFTER had been scrapped while White owned the yard in 1986. KINLOSS had latterly been used by the Naval Construction Research Establishment at Rosyth as a shock test vessel. The hulk of the frigate EASTBOURNE is still there, five years after her arrival in 1985.

Three wooden inshore minesweepers at Pounds yard at Portsmouth in August 1958. Newly delivered inshore minesweepers not required operationally at the time were laid up at the old gunboat yard at Haslar and at a covered facility at Rosneath in the Gareloch. A serious fire at Haslar on 29 September 1956 resulted in the burnt out hulks of BROADLEY (left), EDLINGHAM and BISHAM being sold for scrap in 1957, barely two years after completion.

1990 saw a brief revival in the British shipbreaking industry, with the disposal of former Soviet warships. Destroyers and submarines were hawked around Europe by middlemen channelling hard currency to Russia. One deal involved eight Whiskey class submarines and five destroyers/escorts which were to be scrapped at Blyth on the former Hughes Bolckow site (which had closed in 1980). The submarines were sold for £50,000 each, arriving from the Baltic via Norway on the submersible BOABARGE 7 in tow of BJORN ESKIL on 15 February 1990. The final purchasers were UK based Andover Marine Services assisted by A P Moller's shipbroking division, but the actual demolition was subcontracted to a Kitson Vickers related company, Oceanics (UK) Ltd.

Six of the submarines went into the 'dock' or beaching ground, while two remained at the deepwater berth. This view on 24 March 1990 from the deck of a boat bearing the painted numbers 329/163 shows the two groups of three in the dock at high tide. The right hand boat had 257 painted on the conning tower.

Another view of the beaching ground at Blyth also on 24 March 1990 as the tide falls. The first submarine to be taken in hand is half demolished. There was no clear identity on the submarines. The pendant numbers were mostly painted out, but as the Soviets frequently changed them anyway, there is no means of telling their true identity. The furthest middle one bore the number 357.

Two of the eight Russian Whiskey class submarines being broken up at Blyth in 1990 heel over as the tide falls on 14th May - a near circular hull can rest at almost any angle. The left hand boat had the number 357 painted on the conning tower, though this was probably not its real hull number.

The Russian Riga class escort SKR 63 (Storezhevoy Korabl) alongside at Blyth on 2 June 1990. She had arrived from Murmansk in tow of the Russian tug STAKHANOVETS on 4th May. All guns had been removed from their mounts, as had radar and electronic equipment. Minelaying rails port and starboard required her stern to be broad.

The British submarine SEALION and SKR 63 under demolition at Blyth are seen here on 2 June 1990. SEALION had been partly dismantled at Chatham by RED Enterprises in 1989, and was resold to Andover Marine Services, arriving at Blyth in tow of CORNISHMAN on 28 March 1990. Her ASR1 diesel engines were removed for Devonport Management Limited for possible use in refitting Oberon class submarines. Right shows the view looking aft from SEALION's sonar dome. Left shows the view from SKR 63's mast, with Whiskey 329/163 ahead of SEALION. Both vessels were moved to the dock early in August.

All sorts of unfamiliar submarine structure was revealed as demolition progressed. The aft end of the third Whiskey to be broken up at Blyth reveals traces of her German Type XXI U-boat origins, with twin shaft layout. This view on 21 July 1990 looks like an artist's cutaway drawing, with (visible at right) the aft pressure hull dome, the fairing enclosing the starboard propeller shaft, the single rudder, the stern planes and the starboard aft torpedo tube shutter.

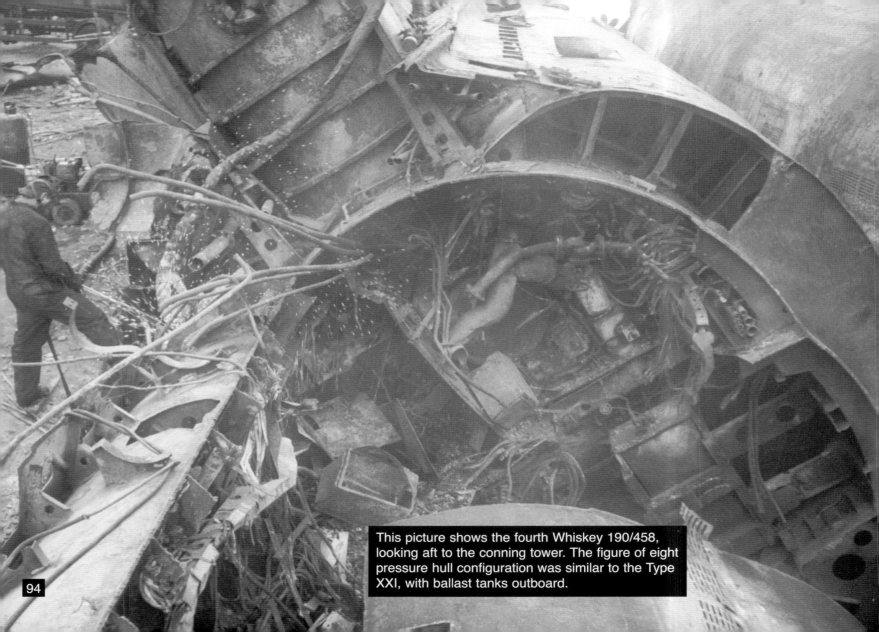

This picture shows the fourth Whiskey 190/458, looking aft to the conning tower. The figure of eight pressure hull configuration was similar to the Type XXI, with ballast tanks outboard.

Faced with falling scrap prices and increasing health and safety demands, Oceanics (UK) departed abruptly from Blyth in June 1991, leaving the half demolished destroyer BYVALY (a 2850-ton mid 1950s built Kotlin destroyer) and the eighth (unidentified) Whiskey seen here on 20 April 1991. Evans of Merseyside finally cleared the hulks for the Blyth Harbour Board in 1992.

INDEX